W9-CAR-821

May 7, 1998

To My Friend Kitty,

Long-lasting friendships
like old quilts become
more valuable with age!
Love,
Kerrie

PATCHWORK OF LOVE

published by Multnomah Books
a part of the Questar publishing family

© 1997 by Questar Publishers, Inc.

International Standard Book Number: 1-57673-074-3

Photography ©1997 by Pamela Hiar, Mike Houska, and Claudia Kunin
Design by D^2 DesignWorks
Quilt research by Cynthia Uttley

Selected quilts © 1997 American Museum of Quilts and Textiles of San Jose.
Use of images does not constitute an endorsement of any kind.

Printed in Hong Kong

ALL RIGHTS RESERVED

No part of this publication may be reproduced, stored in a retrieval system,
or transmitted, in any form or by any means—electronic, mechanical,
photocopying, recording, or otherwise—without prior written permission.

For information:
Questar Publishers, Inc. • Post Office Box 1720 • Sisters, Oregon 97759

LIBRARY OF CONGRESS CATALOGING-IN-PUBLICATION DATA

Patchwork of love / by Questar Publishers.
p.   cm.
ISBN 1-57673-074-3 (alk. paper)
1. Quilts--United States--Psychological aspects. 2. Friendship--Quotations, maxims, etc.   I. Questar Publishers.
NK9112.P38   1997
746.46'0973--dc21   96-40150
CIP

97 98 99 00 01 02 03 04 05 06 — 10 9 8 7 6 5 4 3 2

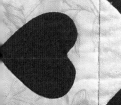

Patchwork of Love

C R E A T I N G   F R I E N D S H I P S
P I E C E   B Y   P I E C E

Heather Harpham Kopp

QUESTAR PUBLISHERS • SISTERS, OREGON

$\mathcal{C}$ontents

Of all the things
a woman's hands have made,
The quilt so lightly thrown
across her bed—
The quilt that keeps her loved ones warm—
Is woven of her love and
dreams and thread.

-CARRIE A. HALL, *THE PATCHWORK QUILT*

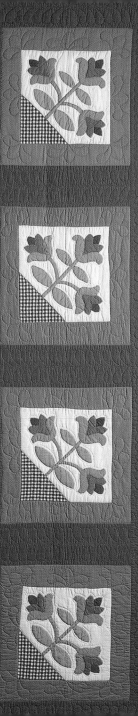

Patchwork of Love

After months, maybe years, of hard work, a quilter often cannot part with her masterpiece for any price. It has gone beyond scraps of material sewn together and become something more—a cherished proof of the rewards of tender investment.

Friendships are like that, too. In fact, quilts can teach us a lot about what a friend is, how much she means to us, and how we can love her. Just as quilts are made with special care and great attention to details, so are the friendships we nurture over time.

Like quilts, friends are created to last a long time; to keep you warm through life's cold winters; to feel good to have nearby. And each one is unique, irreplaceable, priceless.

I hope as you read this book that you will cherish all the more the patchwork of love that you and your friends have sewn into each other's lives.

The laughter of a friend is embroidered with love.
A friend laughs with you
and for you—at knotted secrets, dropped stitches,
and blunders that turned out beautiful.

But she always laughs most freely
at herself.

PART ONE

The Comfort of a Friend

"A friend loves at all times."

-PROVERBS 17:17

The Very Best  Kind of Friend

If you are comfortable with her,
and can plop down in her presence
and feel warm as if by a fire—

And if you cherish the way
her lazy cat purrs,
or the way her peppermint tea soothes
your poor tired throat—

you have found the best
kind of friend.
She is like
the hearth of home.

Sometimes children
make the best friends of all.
With one smile, they tumble color
across a blank swatch
of an ordinary day.

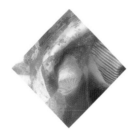

There is no friendship,
no love, like that of the parent for the child.

-HENRY WARD BEECHER

The Crazy Quilt

I have an old quilt made by my father's grandmother. It's not a beautiful quilt, and all the fabric appears to be quite old. But I love it.

The pieces are probably leftover scraps from Aunt Fran's apron, little Mary's Easter dress, or Grampa's favorite shirt. They are odd shapes and sizes. Some nameless shapes have hooks and curves, long slivers of fabric painstakingly sewn with dozens of meticulous stitches. A few tiny patches are smaller than my thumbnail.

Some of the fabric is very plain with dull colors. I can just hear some tired mother say, "But, dear, it's a very serviceable cloth...." while her daughter frowns at the new school dress. Other pieces are bright and cheery, like snippets of birthdays, summer vacations, and fun times gone by. A few fancier pieces are satiny smooth with embossing or embroidery; they seem to whisper of weddings, dances, a first kiss....

My father's grandmother was nearly blind and perhaps that explains why the shades appear haphazardly arranged and almost seem to shout at each other. I wonder if she ever realized what her creations looked like, or did she simply go by touch? They do have an interesting texture—smooth next to bumpy, seersucker alongside velvet; and all over the quilt hundreds of tiny stitches, almost invisible to the eye, pucker ever so slightly.

If I were blind, I would like to make quilts like this.

Recently my own family relocated to a new town, and I was in bed with the flu, wrapped in my great-grandmother's crazy quilt. I felt sorry for myself and I missed the friends I'd left behind. Deep down, I knew it was partly my own fault—I hadn't taken steps to establish new friendships. Several acquaintances seemed willing, but I was holding back, hesitating....

As I studied the crazy quilt, I thought of the many friends I'd had throughout my life. Some felt a bit scratchy and rough like a sturdy piece of wool, but in time they softened—or I became used to them. Others were delicate like silk and needed to be handled with care. Some were colorful and bright and great fun to be with. A few special others felt soft and cozy like flannel, and they knew how to make me feel better.

Many of my friends have only been around for a season. So often I've had to leave them behind, or they leave me! And yet, in my heart, I know they are friends for life. If I met them on the street tomorrow, we would hug and laugh and talk non-stop. It would seem like yesterday.

And that's because God has sewn them into my heart.

I pulled the old quilt closer around me, comforted and warmed by my memories. Surely, my own masterpiece—this quilt of friendships I fretted over—was not nearly finished. I would make new friends in this town. And like my great-grandmother, trusting her fingers to lead her, I would, by faith, reach out.

—MELODY CARLSON

"*Happy is the house that shelters a friend!*"

- EMERSON

Life is like a patchwork quilt
And each little patch is a day,
Some patches are rosy, happy and bright,
And some are dark and gray.

But each little patch as it's fitted in
And sewn to keep it together
Makes a finished block in this life of ours
Filled with sun, and with rainy weather.

So let me work on Life's patchwork quilt
Through the rainy days and the sun—
Trusting that when I have finished my block
The Master may say: "Well done."

-Elizabeth Ryan DeCoursey

A New Creation

When life is lying in shreds,
wasted pieces at your feet,
and your best efforts are scattered
as far as you can see...

only a dear friend can
safely approach.

She enters first with
silence and soft reassurance.

Then she kindly suggests that you
place the orange paisley

alongside your leftover green linen
to create a new design....

You begin again, patiently,
two heads leaning to the task
where only one had worked before....

Later, when redemption
spreads out a new creation
in your hands,
you see a miracle more amazing
than any ever made without
failure—or friend.

Friendship only is,
indeed, genuine when two friends,
without speaking a word to each other, can, nevertheless,
find happiness in being together.

-GEORGE EVERS

When I am with a friend,
I like to listen to her
tell me over and over again,
who she really is.

And when all is said and done,
and her heart is gently hung out
as if to dry in the soft breeze,
I embrace her.

Two can accomplish more than twice as much as one,
for the results can be much better.

-ECCLESIASTES 4:9 (LIVING BIBLE)

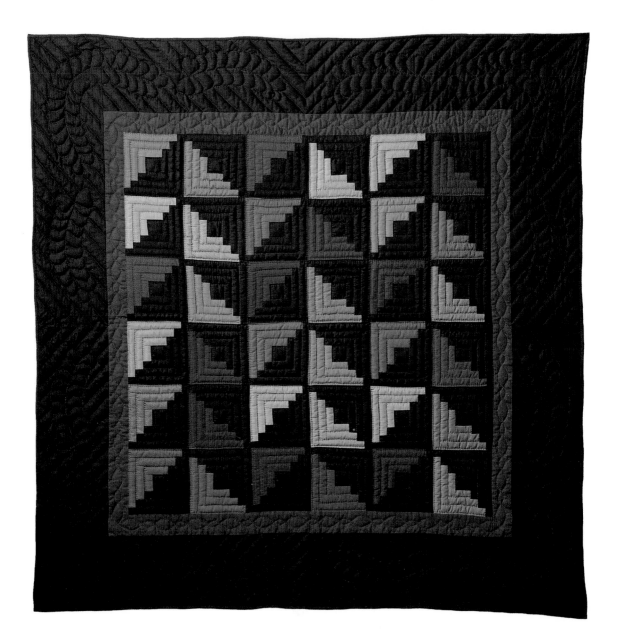

The Log Cabin Quilt

"Before my father died he was a lumberman; we lived in a forest near Lufkin. He built our house. It was a log house and it was plenty big, two fireplaces. He had plans all laid out to make it bigger when the family grew and when he could get the time.

He put such care in fittin' everything just perfect. He always whistled when he worked. Sometimes he and Mama would whistle harmony. We all turned to listen to that when it happened. I was always allowed to choose if I wanted to work outside with Papa or inside with Mama. When I was younger I dearly loved workin' outside with him.

Well, every time I make a Log Cabin I think of him."

— MRS. SMITH IN *THE QUILTERS*

"*A beloved friend*
does not fill one part of the soul,
but, penetrating the whole,
becomes connected with all feeling."

-WILLIAM ELLERY CHANNING

PART TWO

The Fabric of Friendship

*"Dear friends, let us love one another,
for love comes from God."*

-1 JOHN 4:7

The fabric of friendship
is a patchwork of love.
Each stitch loops one life to another,
and holds fast the like and the unlike,
in perfect harmony.

Treat your friends
always as if you had all the time in the world
to enjoy them.

But remember that it's the small moments
which often matter most.

Kindness is a friend's greatest asset.
With it, she can
mend misunderstandings
and smooth out rumpled feelings.
With only a well-placed word,
she can raise a downcast spirit.

The stitches in this quilt-patch rare,
Were patiently made with loving care;
If each thought put forth were as perfect and true,
It would make a grand world for me and you.

-IDA H. FREDERICK

A soulmate believes in your whole unfolding life,
not just the pieces visible now.

When you despair,
she points out the constant threads
of gold among the gray.

Where you see only loss
and confusion,
she reveals a tapestry of love.

The Quilt

Mehetabel Elwell had never felt the pleasure of being important. Not that she was useless in her brother's family; as a matter of course, she took it upon herself to perform the most tedious and uninteresting part of the household labors. And she did not resent doing them.

Her sister-in-law, a big hearty housewife, was rather kind in an absent, offhand way to the shrunken little old woman, and it was through her that Mehetabel was able to enjoy the one pleasure of her life. Even as a girl she had been clever with her needle in the way of patching bed quilts, and in this work she enjoyed at least a small sense of accomplishment.

Sometimes the neighbors would send over and ask "Miss Mehetabel" for such and such a design. It was with an agreeable flutter at being able to help someone that she went to the dresser, in her bare little room under the eaves, and extracted from her crowded portfolio the pattern desired.

She never knew how her great idea came to her. She never admitted to herself that she could have thought of it without other help; it was too great, too ambitious. At first it seemed to her only like a lovely but quite unreal dream. But so curiously does familiarity accustom us even to very wonderful things, that as she lived with this astonishing creation of her mind, the longing grew stronger and stronger to give it material life with her nimble old fingers.

She had but little time from her incessant round of household drudgery for this new and absorbing occupation, and she did not dare sit up late at night lest she burn too much candle. It was weeks before the little square began to take on a finished look, to show the pattern. Then Mehetabel was in a fever of impatience to bring it to completion. Finally, she could wait no longer and one evening ventured to bring her work down beside the fire where the family sat, hoping that some good fortune would give her a place near the tallow candles on the mantelpiece.

Up to that moment, Mehetabel had labored in the purest spirit of disinterested devotion to an ideal, but as Sophia held her work toward the candle to examine it, exclaiming in amazement and admiration, Mehetabel felt an astonished joy to know that her creation would stand the test of publicity.

By the end of summer, family interest had risen so high that Mehetabel was given a little stand in the sitting room where she could keep her pieces and work in odd minutes. She almost wept over such kindness, and resolved firmly not to take advantage of it by neglecting her work, which she performed with a fierce thoroughness.

A year went by and a quarter of the quilt was finished; a second year passed and a half was done. The third year Mehetabel had pneumonia and lay ill for weeks and weeks, overcome with terror lest she die before her work was completed. A fourth year and one could see the grandeur of the whole design; and in September of the fifth year, the entire family watching her with eager and admiring eyes, Mehetabel quilted the last stitches.

The girls held it up by the four corners, and they all looked at it in solemn silence. Then Mr. Elwell smote one horny hand within the other and exclaimed: "By ginger! That's goin' to the county fair!" Mehetabel blushed a deep red. The thought had occurred to her in a bold moment, but she had not dared entertain it.

Even in her swelling pride Mehetabel felt a pang of separation as the bulky package was carried out of the house. As the days went on she felt absolutely lost without her work. For years it had been her one true joy, and she could not bear even to look at the little stand, now quite bare of the litter of scraps which had lain on it so long. The family noticed the old woman's depression, so one day Sophia asked kindly, "You feel sort o' lost without the quilt, don't you, Mehetabel?"

"They took it away so quick!" she said wistfully. "I hadn't hardly had one real good look at it myself."

Mrs. Elwell made no comment, but a day or two

later she asked Mehetabel if she would like to go to the fair.

Mehetabel looked at her with incredulity. It was as though someone had offered her a ride in a golden chariot up to the very gates of heaven. "Why, you can't mean it!" she cried, paling with the intensity of her emotion.

On her return home from the fair the next evening she was very pale, and so tired and stiff that her brother had to carry her into the house. Her lips, however, were set in a blissful smile. The family crowded around her with a throng of questions.

Mehetabel drew a long breath. "It was just perfect!" she said. "Finer even than I thought. They've got it hanging up in the very middle of a sort o' closet made of glass, and one of the lower corners is ripped and turned back so's to show the seams on the wrong side. There are a whole lot of other ones in that room, but not one that can hold a candle to it, if I do say so....

"I went right to the room where the quilt was, and then I didn't want to leave it. It had been so long since I'd seen it. And then the people begun comin' in and I got so interested in hearin' what they had to say I couldn't think of goin' anywheres else. I ate

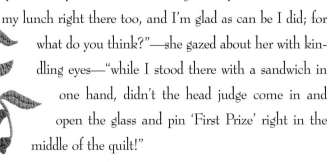

my lunch right there too, and I'm glad as can be I did; for what do you think?"—she gazed about her with kindling eyes—"while I stood there with a sandwich in one hand, didn't the head judge come in and open the glass and pin 'First Prize' right in the middle of the quilt!"

There was a stir of congratulation and proud exclamation. Then Sophia asked, "Didn't you go to see anything else?"

"Why, no," said Mehetabel. "Only the quilt. Why should I?"

She fell into a reverie where she pictured again the glorious creation of her hand and mind hanging before all the world with the mark of highest approval on it. She longed to make her listeners see the splendid vision with her. She struggled for words; she reached blindly after unknown superlatives. "I tell you it looked like—" she said, hesitating. Vague recollections of hymn book phraseology came into her mind, the only form of literary expression she knew; but they were dismissed because saying them might seem sacrilegious and not sufficiently forcible.

Finally, "I tell you it looked real well!" she assured them, and sat staring into the fire, on her tired old face the contented smile of someone, who has, at last, stitched her own special place in the world.

-ADAPTED FROM DOROTHY CANFIELD'S
HILLSBORO PEOPLE, 1915

The Garden, (illustrated on page 38) an appliqué quilt by Piné Lorraine Eisfeller, won first prize for quilting in the 1942 Women's Day National Needlework Contest.

*The hands of time
are kind to those who sew
their love with patience.*

"A word fitly spoken
is like apples of gold
In settings of silver."

-PROVERBS 25:11 (NKJV)

"You know how I got my quilts when I got married? We lived out in the country...and they didn't give showers like they do now. You just had your own hope chest and you had to fill it. I had four quilts when I got married. I quilted three and Mother gave me one. That was enough to start house with. I had to supply all my kids when they got married, and when my sister's house burned, I set her up again with quilts."

-ELIZA CALVERT HALL
IN *AUNT JANE OF KENTUCKY*

Ask a true friend anything at all, and she will look you
in the eye and tell you the truth with mercy.

Ask her nothing at all—
and she will still do the same.

*The friends of your heart
are not to be taken for granted—
and should always be granted
much more than they
would take.*

Square by square,
hour by hour,
a true companion has the power to
make work pass quickly
and love linger long.

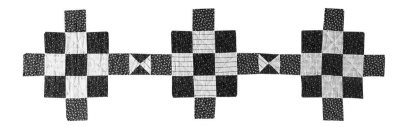

"Make my joy complete
by being of the same mind,
maintaining the same love,
united in spirit,
intent on one purpose."

-PHILLIPIANS 2:2

How unique each of the friends
who have been stitched into my life!
Only God could design a way to piece
all those varied hearts together to create
something so beautiful.

Just as the nails pierced his hands,
so his love pierces our lives
like thread through our souls,
and binds us together
until we are one.

PART THREE

A Lasting Friendship

*"Greater love has no one than this,
that he lay down his life for his friends."*

-JOHN 15:13

Friendship is not so fragile as it seems.
Though corners may unravel,
and stitches loosen,
when two hearts
are joined at the seams,
hardships only strengthen
the affectionate bond between.

Friendship is a long piece of work that,
with faith, will never be finished.

Friends remember every stitch they've
sewn together—or ripped apart.
Mixed in with memories
of laughter and tears,
are the dearest remembrances of all—
the taking of turns at forgiveness.

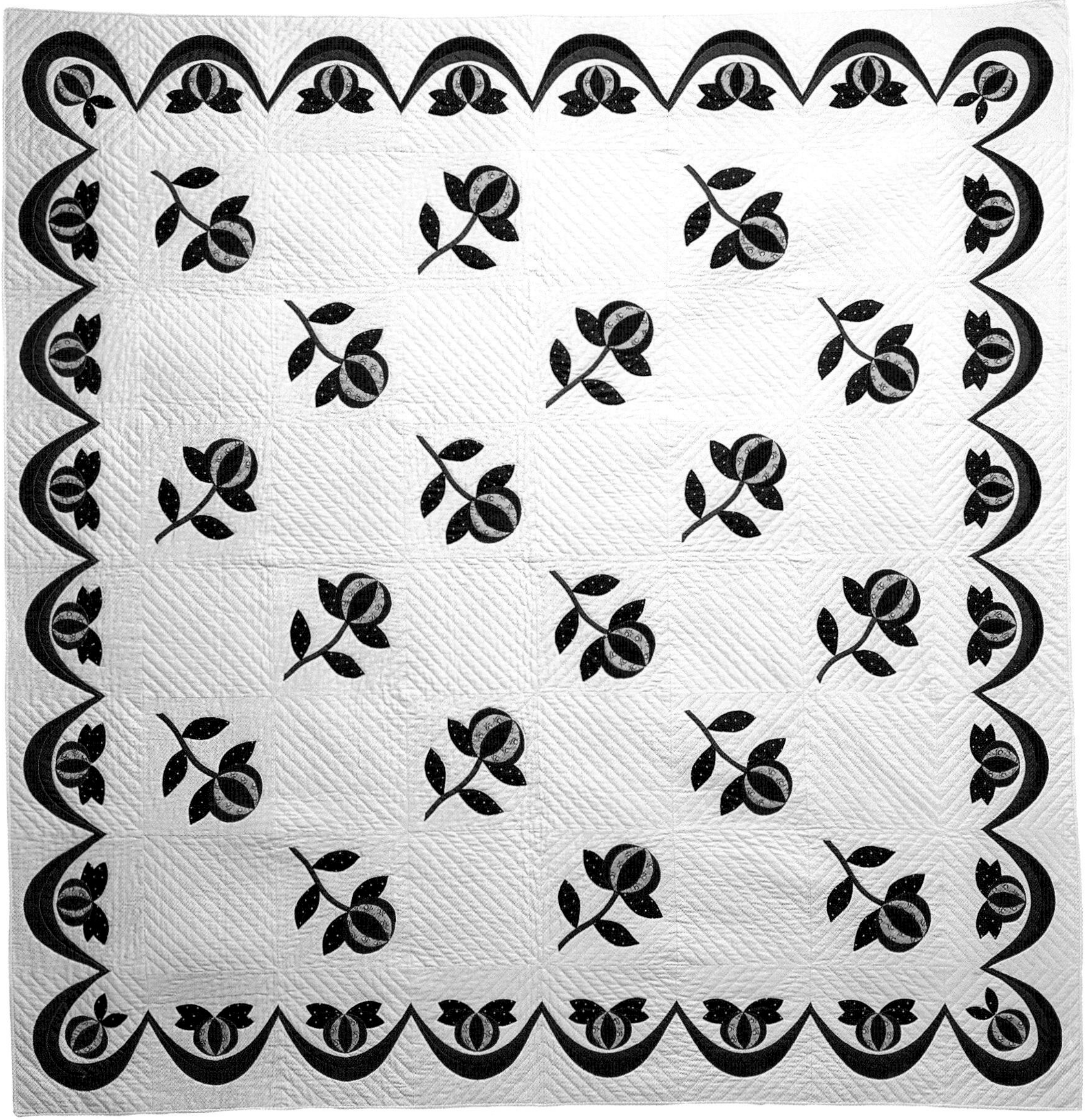

I do not wish
to treat friendships daintily,
but with roughest courage.
When they are real,
they are not glass threads or frostwork,
but the solidest thing
we know.

-RALPH WALDO EMERSON

Every friendship begins small.
Two smiles meet and
hold somehow.

But as each day passes,
amid coffee or tea,
shared secrets and phone calls,
carpools and quilting bees——
a love grows large
enough to last into eternity.

Piecemeal Memories

Cloth. Bags and baskets and boxes of cloth. A gift to me from my uncle who'd found it while cleaning house after my aunt died. Mostly little pieces, the cloth came from my grandmother, maybe my great-grandmother, from cousins, great-aunts, and friends of the family. Scraps my aunt had been meaning, perhaps, to do something with.

So deliberately saved, the scraps must not be wasted. Rumpled and chaotic, they sought order: press me, cut me, piece me, sew me, rescue me! They had waited long enough.

I found lace. I found satin. I found twenty or thirty apron strings, pressed and soft with wear. Who, I wondered, had taken the time to save these after their aprons were stained and worn beyond repair? I pictured the hands, white with flour, slick with lard, that had tied the apron strings. I remembered the bread my grandmother baked every Friday, the sweet, salty butter she churned, the gravy of canned meat she prepared.

Calico, gingham, silk, homespun, wool, rayon, even velvet. Who in our family wore velvet? On what occasion? I found pockets from what looked like the cotton house-dresses my grandmother used to wear. I found remnants of homemade curtains and remembered the rooms in which they had hung. I even found scraps from my own teenage foray into dressmaking: a green jumper made in a high school home economics class (and for which I'd received a disappointing C+). I found the cutoff hem of a purple wool hand-me-down skirt I'd shortened according to the breezy fashion of the day. Somebody—my aunt, my mother, my grandmother—had saved these bits and pieces of my life. I held memory between my thumb and index finger; I relived adolescence in the texture of the threads.

Then I began to cut scrap after scrap into one-inch squares, sorting them into envelopes by color. I cut yards of muslin into twelve-inch squares. I began to sew, by hand, the small squares onto the big ones, learning as I went about small, even stitches, straight lines, crisp corners.

So far, I've finished six squares and pieced together almost a thousand "postage stamps." I work in spurts between other sewing projects. I work when the mood strikes, when the house is quiet, when the conversation slows. I work while watching television and with my best sewing friends at our Wednesday night women's club.

Mine is, I have realized, a lifelong commitment. Of course, when I've created enough squares to assemble a twin, queen, king size quilt, whatever, I will assemble them. I enjoy closure. I am sewing my way to closure. But when this quilt is finished, I will start another. The process continues.

This summer I made a Bargello quilt for my daughter and contributed two squares to a friendship quilt—which generated new scraps for my collection and will be reduced, eventually, to "postage stamps." My friend Carolyn, at work on a Grandmother's Flower Garden, sends me pinks and blues from Maine. Sarah—who used to be my neighbor and is still my favorite partner in gossip—is also making a postage-stamp quilt. She sends her favorite reds, teals, and blacks from San Francisco. Jane and Pet, my women's club compatriots, also contribute regularly.

The knowledge that my scrap bag will never be empty comforts me. I imagine that someday my child, or grandchild, or great-grandchild will find the scraps I leave behind and wonder who took the trouble to save them and why. Perhaps—out of nostalgia or curiosity or a genetically predetermined need for closure and wholeness, to use and to be of use—that child will slip a thimble on her finger and take up a needle and thread.

Perhaps she, too, will sew secrets into her squares—one royal-blue solid among the flowered pastels, a camouflaged diamond, a circle of hope, dark disappointment, a modified rainbow. Memories and surprises for the discerning eye.

—REBECCA RULE

Far and near I sought
Utterance in a thought
A garden ever blooming, just for you;

So flowers that will not wilt
I stitched into a quilt,
My treasure-trove of memories
for you.

-JOSEPHINE DAY MICKLESON

A favorite friend is like
an old treasured quilt,
that gets more cozy,
more warm and familiar,
the more
it gets used.

*"Be slow in choosing a friend,
slower in changing."*

-BENJAMIN FRANKLIN

God made friends
because He couldn't be here like
a blanket wrapped around us

every morning

The place
where two friends first met
is sacred to them all through their friendship,
all the more sacred as their friendship
deepens and grows old.

-PHILLIP BROOKS

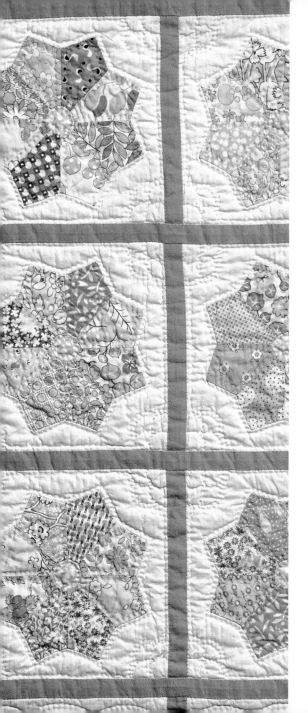

"When I was about four years old
the neighbor's baby died, and all
the women were called in to help.
Mama knew what her part was
because right away she took some
blue silk out of her hope chest.
Mama and three other women set
up the frame and quilted all day.
First they quilted the lining for the
casket, and then they made a tiny
little quilt out of the blue silk to
cover the baby."

—LOIS HAND IN *THE QUILTERS*

Our souls are like children.
They need to know where home is, who to trust,
and how to get a hug.
No wonder God made friends.

Friendship is a long,
sweet prayer
made up of kind acts that
reach heavenward.

Quilts

Notes

Untitled poems by Elizabeth Ryan DeCoursey, Ida H. Frederick, and Josephine Day Mickleson from *The Romance of the Patchwork Quilt in America* by Carrie A. Hall. Used with permission of the Caxton Printers, Ltd., Caldwell, Idaho.

"Piecemeal Memories" by Rebecca Rule. Excerpted / Condensed by permission from the March 1993 issue of *Country Living,* © 1993 by the Hearst Corporation.

Quotes by Hattie Wooddell, Lois Hand, and Mrs. Smith from *The Quilters: Women and Domestic Art* by Patricia Cooper and Norma Bradley Buferd, © 1977 by Patricia Cooper Baker and Norma Bradley Buferd. Used by permission of Doubleday, a division of Bantam Doubleday Dell Publishing Group, Inc.

"The Quilt" by Dorothy Canfield. Excerpted / Condensed from *Hillsboro People,* Henry Holt and Co. 1915.